Children of
Appalachia

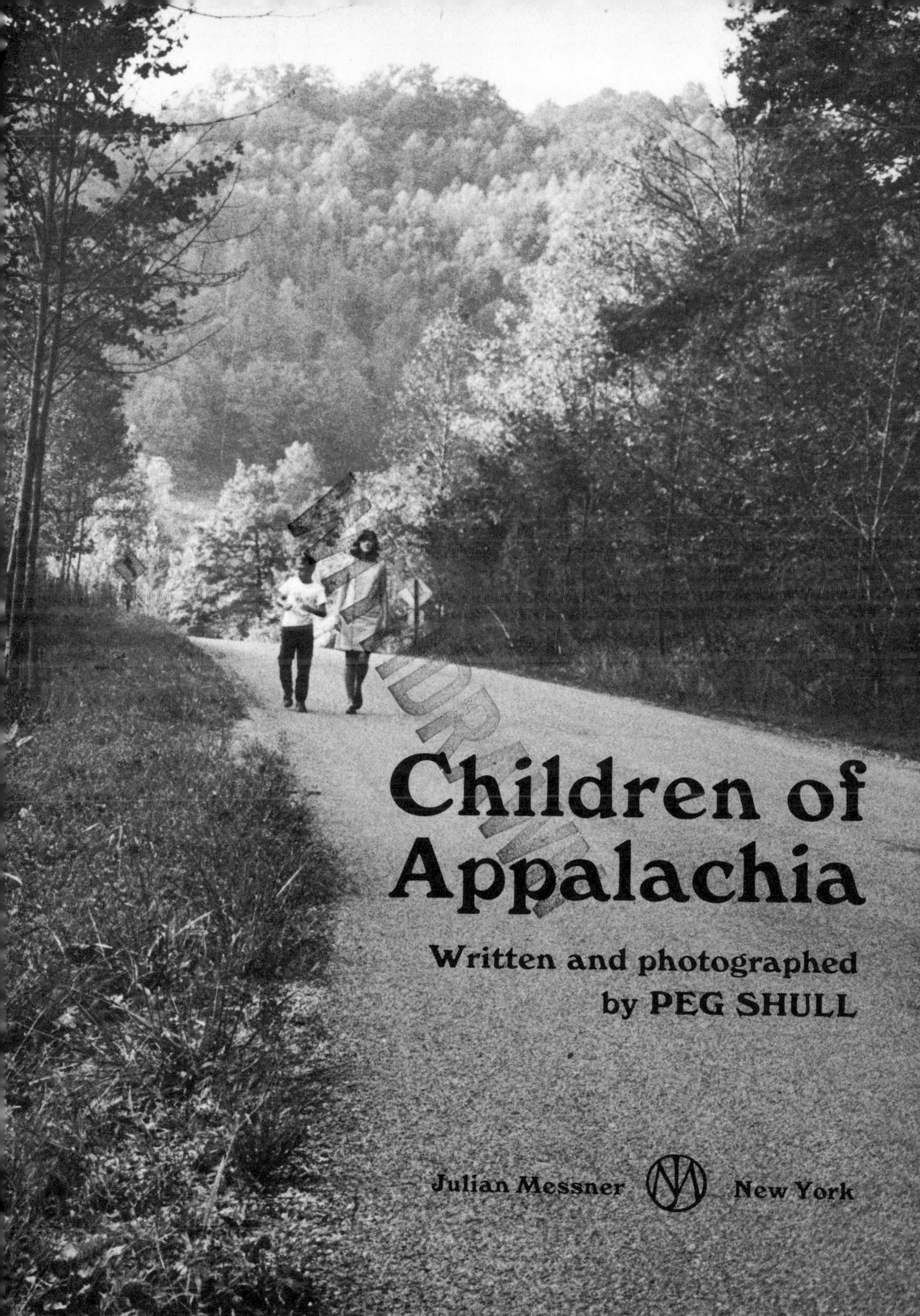

Children of Appalachia

Written and photographed
by PEG SHULL

Julian Messner   New York

Published simultaneously in the United States and Canada by
Julian Messner, a division of Simon & Schuster, Inc.,
1 West 39 Street, New York, N.Y. 10018. All rights reserved.

Copyright, ©, 1969 by Margaret Wyse Shull

Printed in the United States of America
SBN 671-32133-1 Trade
SBN 671-32134-X MCE
Library of Congress Catalog Card No. 79-81386
Design by Marjorie Zaum K.

*For the good people I met in Bell County, Kentucky—
especially Jim Shull*

Author's Note

The facts in *Children of Appalachia* were gathered through observation and personal interviews while I was a reporter for a Bell County, Kentucky, newspaper and while shooting the photos for this book in the fall of 1968.

Children of Appalachia is an attempt to show life in southeastern Kentucky, both the good and the bad, as it is. The families in this book are composites, with features of both the people and their homes taken from several families throughout the county. The names Napier, Sizemore, and Begley are common in the mountains, but not in Bell County. Some features attributed to Red Bird Mission are in Henderson Settlement, another United Methodist Church mission in Bell County.

I am grateful to Maurice K. Henry, publisher of the Middlesboro *Daily News,* and to the Reverend Dr. John Bischoff, director of Red Bird Mission, for their reading of the manuscript, and to my friends in Bell County who allowed me to photograph them in their homes and at work, often at inconvenient times, and who both advised and fed me and my family. They prefer to remain nameless, but cannot be forgotten.

P.S.
New York City
October 21, 1968

Contents

Children of
Appalachia

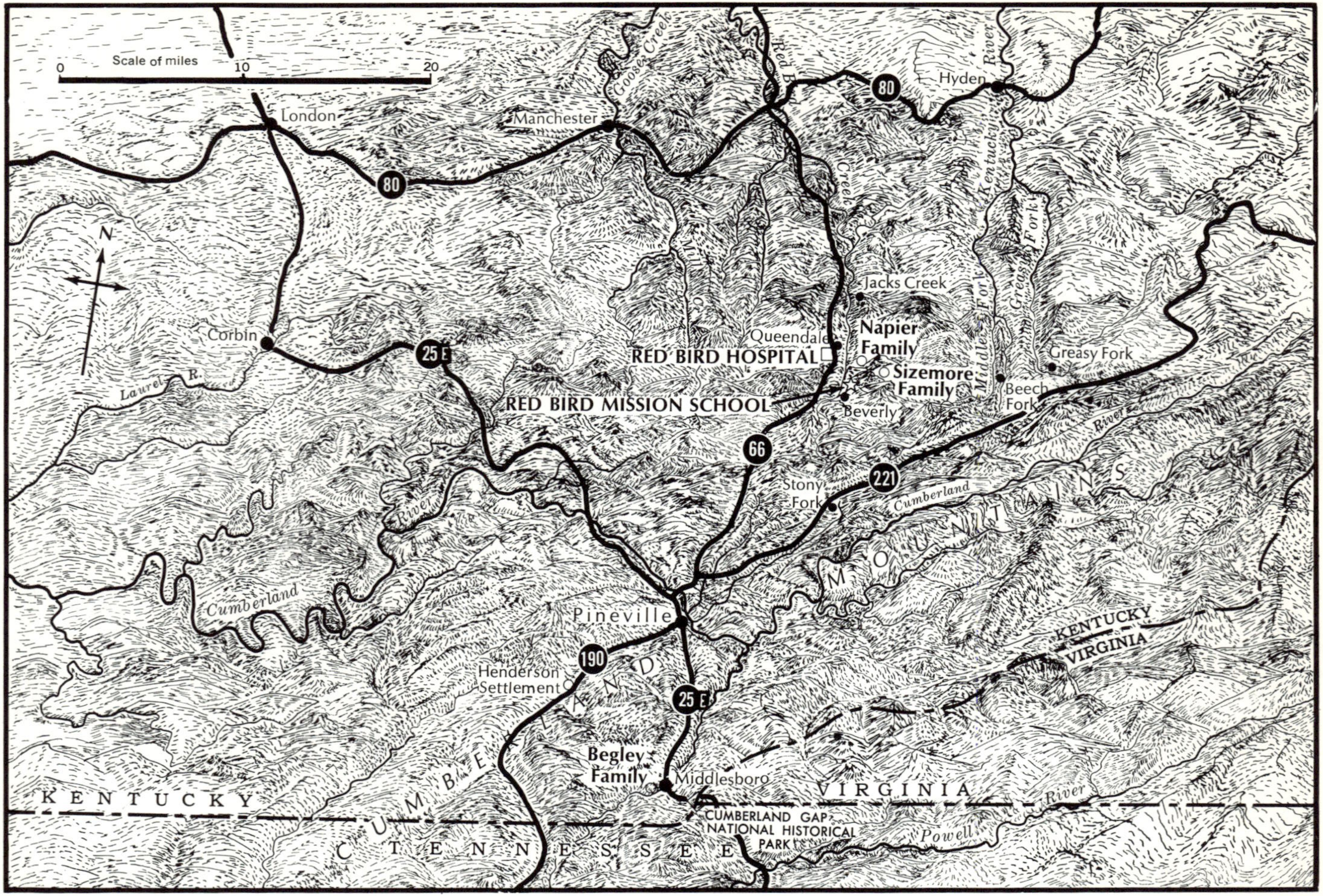

Map by William Jaber

CHAPTER 1

The Farm
on
Red Bird
Creek

The Napier family wakened before dawn. Haying was finished. The tobacco was safely hanging in the barn. But school had started so ten-year-old Bill and his older sisters Nancy and Margaret had to get up early to help with the chores.

Their farm is large for the mountains, over a hundred acres. Nearly seventy-five acres are flat enough for crops and livestock. The rest is covered with timber, which can be harvested for a few trees a year.

The Napiers live in northern Bell County, Kentucky. Their mailing address is Beverly, which is only a country store combined with a post office. A mile down the road is the main Red Bird Mission school.

This region is in the heart of the Appalachian Mountains, which begin in eastern Canada and end in Alabama. Locally, the mountains are called the Cumberlands. This is just one part of the area newspapers and the federal government call Appalachia.

Many people in Appalachia are poor. There are several reasons for this. The most important reason is that they have poor land. The Napier farm, however, is on rich bottomland that has been flattened and watered by Red Bird Creek. But farms farther up the mountains, where the many creeks become smaller, have little land flat enough for planting large crops or raising cattle.

For many years, coal mining has been an important industry in eastern Kentucky. But some careless men who manage coal companies have often ripped the mountains apart to take out the coal. Then they have not replaced the soil, trees, and grass. This is most true of strip mines. Strip miners rip the top layers of soil and rock off the mountain. Then they take out the coal underneath. At first, miners often did not replace the soil and plants. When soil and plants are not replaced, the rain washes the rich topsoil down into the creeks. This leaves only poor soil, which makes it difficult for plants to grow again. Now the government says the miners must replace soil and plant new trees.

A coal mine in eastern Kentucky. The main part of the mine is buried in the surrounding mountains.

Some houses with their patched roofs barely keep out the wind.
The creek runs through the front yard, and the land which is on
the mountains is too steep to farm.

The Napiers, and many families like them, have a good life. Mr. Napier studied farming at the University of Kentucky. Bill, Nancy, and Margaret plan to go to college, at least for a year or two. Because they are good students, most of their expenses probably will be paid by scholarships. But even with scholarships, most families cannot afford more years of school. The older people also doubt its value, and the younger ones become lonesome when they are away from the mountains.

Mountain people rarely want to leave the mountains. Some do leave, looking for better jobs or to go to school. But they are unhappy and feel insecure in flat country. Seeing the mountains all around makes them feel safe and protected. The mountains seem to defend them from the outside world they see on their television sets.

Bill shivered in the early morning darkness. He

A scarred mailbox with a cigarette tin taking the place of a missing flag, a wrecked car, and highway signs showing that the road is going to curve are part of the way Appalachia looks.

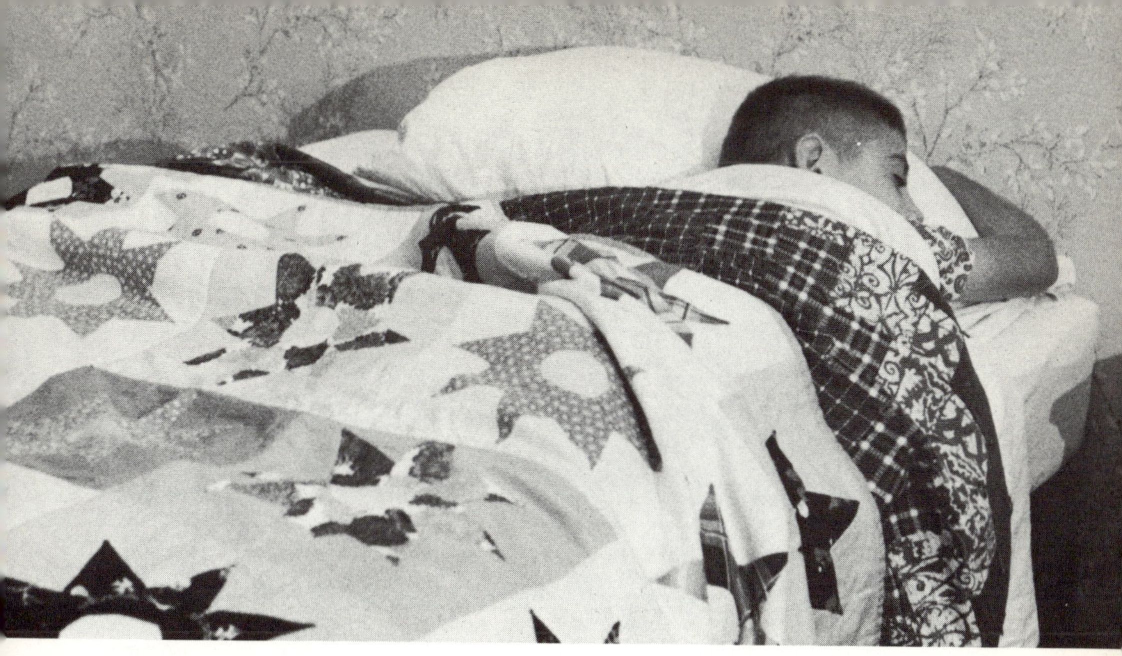

Bill Napier wakens under the patchwork quilts made by his mother.

threw back the two lightweight cotton patchwork quilts and hopped out of bed. Before spring came, it might take four or five quilts to keep him warm. Grabbing his work clothes, he trotted to the warmer bathroom to dress. Before he could run out of the kitchen door, his mother saw him barefooted and made him put on shoes.

"That's silly. It's warm in September," he told Boots, the farm dog. "When the sun's higher, it'll be warm. I won't need shoes till November—well, late October—except for school and church." Boots wagged his tail in agreement as he followed Bill to the barn.

"Hey, Bill, get the gate." Mr. Napier was driving

The Napiers' barn holds twenty-five cattle and two thousand bales of hay.

the ten dairy cows into the milking parlor. It was new and still smelled of fresh lumber. The cattle barn behind it was only five years old. It had been built from plans Mr. Napier got from the university. The loft held two thousand bales of hay and was overflowing. That hay would feed the stock through the winter.

Milking in the new parlor was very modern. The cows were milked by machine. The milk went through tubes to the cooler, then the dairy truck, without being touched. Even so, a few drops trickled down to the waiting barn cats.

Bill's chores led him to the barn that housed the thirty hogs. Most of them were outside because of the mild weather. He fed them first, then went into the barn. From the rafters hung the newly cut tobacco. It would be left to dry until late October, before the first frost, when the leaves would have wilted and softened.

Then they would be stripped from the stalks, taken to market, and sold at auction.

The hog barn was older than the cow barn, but it had been modernized. New farrowing pens, where the pigs were born, were made with concrete floors. The pens had special places where the little pigs, or shoats, could crawl so the mother hog would not lie on them. These pens save many shoats from being crushed and thus help the farm make money.

Bill first fed the sow who had a new litter of twelve shoats. Then he fed the other sows; the gelts, hogs that were being fattened to sell; and finally the prize Yorkshire boar.

Bill fed a sick beef cow that was being kept in the barn. Then by the time he fed Jake, the mule, his stomach was saying it was time for breakfast. As he ran back to the house, there wasn't a cloud in the sky.

Bill pours water into the hogs' trough. Their food is poured into the top of the semi-automatic feeder where they are eating.

Bill feeds one of the cows in the barn. The tall silo holds ears of corn until they are needed during the winter and the spring.

The trees were turning red and yellow.

"What a day for hunting, Boots!" he yelled. The dog leaped after him. There were rabbits, squirrels, and other small animals on the mountain. Sometimes, Bill could even see deer tracks. Boots was ready for hunting, but Bill had to go to school.

Bill washed, then put on clean slacks, a shirt, socks, and shoes. As he was combing his hair, he heard his mother calling the men—him and his father—to breakfast. Then he heard his father come in from milking.

"Margaret made the biscuits today," his mother

said as they sat at the table. "Now she's sixteen, I reckon she's old enough."

"I'll be glad when I'm sixteen," twelve-year-old Nancy said.

Bill piled biscuits on his plate. Then he reached for the scrambled eggs and his mother's specially cured sausage. He covered them all with gravy, then carefully tried a biscuit. "Say, Sis, these aren't bad," he said.

"Thanks," Margaret said, blushing with pleasure.

"Pa, will we be going to town Saturday?" Margaret asked. Town meant Pineville, the county seat, fifteen miles southwest.

"I need to get a uniform since I'm starting to work at the hospital."

"Oh, yes, Pa. Let's go. Please," Bill and Nancy chimed in.

"Don't worry your pa this morning." Their

Mrs. Napier guides Margaret as she makes the morning biscuits. Nancy watches.

mother's voice was sharp. "He was out most of the night."

The children were ashamed. They had not heard the shortwave radio calling the volunteer firemen, nor had they heard their father leave.

"Was the fire bad, Pa?" Margaret asked. "Where was it?"

"Tom Sizemore's. His wife was burned right smart. They took her to the hospital."

"Not Dan's ma?" Bill asked. Dan Sizemore had been his best friend since school started three weeks ago.

"No, they're cousins, I reckon. These live just past Beverly. The house wasn't burned much. They'll be able to mend it in a few days."

Before the volunteer fire department, and the paved roads the fire trucks could travel on, the house would have burned to the ground. The fire department was informal, but it worked. The first man to answer the alarm drove the fire truck. His wife would call the others by shortwave radio. Some other men would reach the fire and be working before the truck arrived.

"We'll probably go to town Saturday, Sister," Mr. Napier said. "Now you kids run or you'll miss the school bus."

CHAPTER 2

Red Bird Mission

Bill got his books and ran out the front door, followed by Nancy and Margaret. They crossed the footbridge over Red Bird Creek, which ran between the house and the road. Then Bill put his books down by the school bus stop and began to look for arrowheads. He had looked all up and down this part of the creek before, but sometimes a rain like the one the night before turned up new arrowheads. They might have belonged to Chief Red Bird himself. That Cherokee chief had hunted deer and wild turkeys along this very stream two hundred years ago.

Bill liked to think about Red Bird. The chief was a real hunter. So were the Long Hunters, like Daniel

side. The Jeep is the only school bus that can reach the children who live high up the creeks, away from roads. Lots of times, Dan wouldn't be there. Today, Bill saw him, though. He waved and yelled.

"Guess what!" Dan said as he sat down. "Pa said you could come spend next weekend with us. Not this —I'm still puttin' in tobacco—but next. Did you ask your folks if it'd be okay?"

"Yeah," Bill said. "Next weekend will be fine. We're going to Pineville this Saturday, I reckon. Can we really go deer hunting?"

"We can hunt them," Dan chuckled. "Whether we'll catch any, I couldn't say. We're bound to catch some squirrels, though, and maybe rabbits. And maybe a deer. You never can tell. One of my brothers got one last year. How we ate!"

Before they had finished talking about hunting, the bus crossed the creek and entered the school yard

A bus arrives at Red Bird School. The metal building at the right houses the gymnasium and metal working shops.

at Red Bird Mission. The grade school and high school are in one large, wooden building. On the left of it is the church. On the right is the gym building, which has woodworking and metalworking shops in the basement. Farther away are the dormitories and administration buildings.

Red Bird is the largest of the six schools that are run as a part of the United Methodist Church mission. It is located about twenty miles northeast of Pineville, Kentucky.

Some of the boys and girls who attend the school are from too far back in the hills for the Jeeps and buses to reach their homes in bad weather. A few are orphans. So these children live in the school dormitories during the school year. Parents are supposed to pay for both their children's attending the school and living in the dorms. But few of them can afford more than a part of the fees, so they pay what they can. The rest is paid by the church or by donations from people outside the area.

There are county public schools in this region, but they are located near the larger towns. If it weren't for the mission schools, a child from the Red Bird area might have to travel two hours or more to and from school.

The main school building at Red Bird Mission is more than fifty years old. At first, its wall were paneled in dark wood. Now, most of the walls have been covered with white plaster.

Bill and Dan's classroom is new. It was added to the third floor four years ago. It is a cheerful room with many windows, and has new desks and maps on the walls.

Miss Heaton, the teacher, looked at her students as they took their seats. Most of them had blonde or light, sandy-colored hair and blue eyes. Others had red hair. Some had black hair and high cheekbones. When she had first arrived, she had guessed that some of their great-grandparents had been Cherokee Indians. She learned later that this was true. She learned, too, that so many children looked alike because nearly all were related to each other. They were descendants of Scots and English pioneers who settled in the mountains even before America became a nation.

As the children took their seats, Miss Heaton thought of how one of them had answered a question the day before.

"I'd just as lief," he said, meaning he'd rather.

"I made the least 'un a play-pretty," a little girl told her, meaning she had made the youngest child in her family a toy.

Polly raises her hand to answer Miss Heaton's question. This room is a recent addition to the old school building.

These expressions, common in Scotland two hundred years ago, had been used generation after generation.

"We'll start with history this morning," Miss Heaton said. "Who can tell me who Richard Henderson was?"

Polly raised her hand. She always knew the answers.

"All right, Polly."

"Richard Henderson was a lawyer. He bought Kentucky from the Indians in 1775."

"Which Indians?" Miss Heaton asked.

"The Cherokees," another girl answered. "Their leader was Attakulluculla, or the Little Carpenter. But

Bill and Dan study together in the school library.

his son, Dragging Canoe, didn't like it. He didn't think the white man had any business buying their land."

"What do you think about that, Dan?" Miss Heaton asked.

"I don't think the Indians were paid enough," Dan said. "Two thousand English pounds and another ten thousand pounds worth of supplies looked like a lot. But by the time it was divided, some Indians only got a shirt or two. They could have gotten more from a day's hunting." Dan always got back to hunting. He wished he had lived in those days when the mountains were filled with deer and wild turkeys.

Bill raised his hand. "Chief Red Bird tried to drive the settlers away until the beginning of the nineteenth

31

Margaret and Bill walk toward the hospital after school. It's a long walk from school, but by going across country their home isn't far from the hospital.

century. But the Indians lost in the end, and went farther west."

The history lesson went on and was followed by a geography lesson until the noon recess.

Bill was surprised when his sister Margaret came up to him at lunch.

"Come with me to see the hospital after school, will you?" she asked. "Nancy was going with me, but she had to stay to sign up for choir."

He could see that it was important to her, because she hardly ever talked to him at school. "Okay," he said. "But I have to be home for chores."

"I do, too," she replied. "I just want you to see

where I'll be working. They're letting me earn enough to pay for my first year of nursing school, after I graduate in June.

After school, Bill and Margaret started walking toward the mission hospital in Queendale. Queendale is the next flat land down the creek from Beverly. The hospital there, like all the schools in the area, is managed by the missionaries of the United Methodist Church.

It was a long walk to the hospital. Bill kept reminding himself that once they got there it was less than a mile home, across the mountain. Soon, a car stopped by them. They looked up to see the mission director, the Reverend Dr. John Bischoff.

"Hop in," he said. "I'll bet you're going to inspect the hospital. I'm going right past there on my way to the sorghum plant," he said. Then he chuckled. "You know, the creeks used to raise Cain all around here. Now, they raise cane, sugarcane, for the plant to turn into sorghum. Your dad owns a little stock in the plant."

"Lots of folks do, don't they?" Margaret asked. "It only costs a few dollars a share."

"That's right," he said. "It's a way for folks to help themselves, even if they only have five or ten dollars to invest. Well, here you are. Have a good look around. I'm really glad you're interested in nursing, Margaret."

The hospital looked small against Chigger Mountain. Bill looked at the building hard, as if he had never seen it before. He had stayed in it twice—when he had his tonsils taken out and when he had broken his arm. But he had never really thought about it.

"This hospital serves ten thousand people, living up to twenty miles away in every direction," Margaret was saying. They walked across the creek on the concrete bridge, across the parking lot, and through the front door. There they were met by the nurse who was going to show Margaret the hospital.

As they followed the nurse, Bill watched his sister with new interest. Margaret was quiet, as always, but her face glowed. Bill could see nothing exciting about a hospital. It was a place to go when you were sick; a place to be avoided. But Margaret seemed to enjoy even the funny smells.

They went through the hospital to the large outpatient clinic. "This is where you try to keep folks from getting sick, isn't it?" Margaret asked shyly.

"Exactly," said the nurse. "When people come in for shots and checkups, we can keep them healthy, or treat an illness before it's too bad. That makes them feel better and makes less work for us, too. But so many

Red Bird Hospital looks small nestled in between Chigger Mountain and Red Bird Creek. It has thirty-one beds and a large outpatient clinic now, and is being enlarged.

people are afraid of a hospital, it's hard to get them to come in."

"I can make them less afraid," Margaret said quietly. "They know I'm one of them, so when I go around telling them about the hospital they'll listen to me. That's one of the things I most want to do. And I want to help more folks get health insurance so they can afford to pay. That's one reason they won't come in. They're proud and they haven't the money."

"How do you know all this, Margaret?" Bill asked.

"I just sort of listen," she said.

"You're the kind of person who should make a good nurse," the nurse said. "We need more people who 'just sort of listen.' This is a wonderful place for a nurse, Margaret, because here you can see how much good you're doing. A lot of the people who come to Red Bird Hospital would die before they could get to one of the towns. A nurse here really feels like she's helping people."

"It means even more, I think, when they're your kin," Margaret said thoughtfully. "There's hardly a soul around here who doesn't share a grandparent with Ma and Pa. They're my people and I want to help make this a better place to live."

The nurse finished the tour as they passed through the drugstore and the laboratory. Looking at Margaret,

Bill knew he would never be afraid of the hospital again. I'll bet she'll make other folks less afraid, too, he thought to himself.

Margaret's face still glowed as they told the nurse good-by and thanked her. "I can hardly wait to work here," she said.

As they started home, Margaret walked slowly and was even quieter than usual. The sun was already hanging low over Chigger Mountain.

"I've got to hurry to feed the animals before it gets dark," Bill said, and he began to walk faster. "Come on, Margaret, hurry."

"I'm coming," she said. "But I love watching the sun set. I don't know how I can leave next fall to go to school in Lexington. I know I have to, though."

"You'll come back, won't you, Sister?" Bill asked.

"Of course, silly," she replied. "You couldn't pay me to stay away."

CHAPTER 3

A Trip
To Town

The Napiers rose even earlier than usual on Saturday morning. Bill and his father finished the feeding and milking, and before noon the chores were done. Then they all piled into the car for the half-hour drive to town.

The haze was beginning to burn off the mountains. On most mornings, it is foggy along the creeks. Usually the weather will clear by midmorning, but sometimes dampness and fog last for several days, especially in cold weather.

"It'll clear; it'll be a fine day," Mr. Napier said.

Most of the road to Pineville, Kentucky Highway 66, is paved with asphalt. The rest is gravel. Some potholes, where last winter's ice had eaten out part of the surface, had not yet been repaired. The road is lumpy with patches over the other holes and cracks.

"It's nice to have a road," Mrs. Napier said. "You children don't remember, but the trip to town used to take a whole day on horseback."

The road wound through the mountains, following the creeks. Not many of the farms they passed were as fertile or as well tended as the Napiers'.

The autumn colors of the trees made the mountains on either side of the road beautiful. As they rounded a bend, the Napiers saw the first of many huge slap heaps. These are piles of the waste which is stripped from the coal as it is mined. They look like a giant's abandoned sand pile. Nothing grows on slag heaps, and they ruin the land beneath them as well.

Mr. Napier snorted, without looking at them. "Coal. The curse of the mountains."

"And their blessing as well," Mrs. Napier added quietly. "Coal is the greatest wealth we have. It has given men jobs; heated lots of houses."

Coal has been both a help and a disadvantage to the mountains. It heats most mountain homes. It makes power for people and factories far from Appalachia. Its mines have given many men jobs. Jobs in the coal mines paid very little at first.

Most coal mines are tunnels, and for many years they were not braced properly. Miners were killed or crippled when the mines caved in.

Then labor unions came into the mountains. A labor union is a group of men who try to get better

Dead trees rise from the slag heaps alongside the road. Slag is the waste from coal mining, and nothing will grow on it.

working conditions and higher wages. The United Mine Workers of America got higher wages for the miners and helped make the mines safer. But when the owners felt the miners were demanding too much pay, they found ways to use more machines in the mines. So many men who were mine workers are now without jobs. Those who are working are well-paid, skilled workers.

Largely because of unemployment among the miners, the United States government has tried in several ways to make life easier for the people of Appalachia. One way is a welfare program whereby the people who cannot find work are given money. Another program sells food stamps to poor people. A dollar's worth of food stamps will buy several dollars' worth of food. Because they are paying for the stamps,

The sign on a grocery store window announces that the owner will take food stamps instead of cash for groceries.

A food stamp, or coupon, rests in the cash register. This one is for fifty cents; another common amount is for two dollars.

the people are not ashamed. They are ashamed of taking charity.

Some of the mountain people are too proud to take government help, even when they need it. Some would even rather go hungry than ask for food stamps. Others only take help until they can find other work. Many, though, soon find how easy it is to live without working. These people keep depending on the government or charity for money and teach their children to do the same.

"It's the folks who won't try that make me wonder about the government programs," said Mr. Napier as he drove toward town. "I don't like to think of anyone's kids going hungry. There's good in these government programs. But they take a man's pride, and that's death to us mountain people. Once a man's pride is gone, he won't work if he can get by on handouts."

They passed a coal tipple. There, coal is dumped from trucks into a chute that sorts the different sizes and sends them down to waiting train cars. The tipple was not working on Saturday, but would be on Monday. The working tipple is a sign that coal is helping the mountain people.

Finally, the road went across a one-lane bridge over the Cumberland River. There it joined the wider, smoother Harlan Road. Soon the Napiers were passing

This tipple sorts different sizes of coal and dumps them into freight cars.

the floodwall that protects Pineville from the river.

Until recently, spring floods rose into mountain towns and did great damage. Nearly all of the towns now have flood walls to keep out all but the worst floods.

"Drop the girls and me at the square," said Mrs. Napier. "We'll have to shop for nurse's aides' uniforms for Margaret and a new skirt for Nancy. Then I'll look around at fabric and things. You can meet us at the A & P in two hours."

Pineville is mainly a farming center, with 3,400 people living there. It is the county seat, meaning the county courthouse is there. The sheriff, tax collector, school superintendent, and county judge have their offices in the courthouse. It is a stone building which looks a little like a castle. It is in the center of town, for Pineville is built around the courthouse square. Stone steps lead to double doors on each side of the building. Shade trees are all around it.

On one corner of the square is the building housing the city hall and fire department. Across the street from it is the town's one hotel. Pineville has a great deal of tourist traffic because U.S. 25E is the main north-south route in that part of the country. Tourism is one of the most important ways people earn their living. Most tourists stay in the several motels on the highway, or at the lodge in Pine Mountain State Park at the edge of town.

Across the one-lane bridge, the road from Red Bird joins the wider Harlan Road on its way into Pineville.

A main street in Pineville, Kentucky.

An outdoor drama, *The Book of Job,* draws many tourists to Pineville in July and August. The drama and the Mountain Laurel Festival, which is a beauty contest, are two of the park's biggest events.

Mrs. Napier and the girls got out of the car at the corner by the hotel. As the car pulled away, they walked down the block past a restaurant toward the dress and fabric shops on the south side of the square.

Bill and his father went to the veterinarian's office first. There, Mr. Napier asked the vet to come and Bang's test his cows. Bang's disease, or brucellosis, is one of the most dreaded diseases among cattle. Because it is very contagious, it can wipe out an entire herd. Therefore, a veterinarian is called in regularly to test the herd for it. Bill listened while his father and the vet discussed feed, vaccinations, and milk production.

Next, they went to the county farm agent's office in the basement of the courthouse. Bill glanced through the hundreds of pamphlets from the U.S. Department of Agriculture and the University of Kentucky while his father and the agent talked.

"I thought you might have heard something more about the plan to straighten the creek," he heard his father say.

Finally, he heard his father's usual closing— "Well, keep us in mind if you hear about anything new" —and knew it was time to go.

"What should I take my wife today?" Mr. Napier asked the county agent's secretary. "She's always right tickled when I bring her a new recipe pamphlet."

"How about tomatoes and honey this week?" the girl asked. She handed him two pamphlets. "I think

The Bell County Courthouse in Pineville.

these have some new recipes you haven't given her yet."

"Well, I'll take your word. I don't know about cooking," he said, and took the pamphlets she offered.

As they walked across the yard, Mr. Napier said, "I know its dull for you, Bill. But a farmer never knows enough nowadays. The county agent can tell you about new drugs or fertilizers, or a better way to build a barn. He can help you farm better, and nowadays it takes the best you can do to make a living. Now would you like an ice cream soda?"

"I'd like that, Pa, but first could we look at the guns at the hardware store?"

Mr. Napier looked serious. "We'll look at guns all you want, Bill," he said. "But I want you to know that you can't have one. I'll let you shoot mine when I'm with you—when I load it and I'm watching everything you do. But I've known boys older than you to get killed with their guns—or their fathers'. Who'd take over the farm when I'm too old if that happened to you?"

"Nothing's going to happen to me, Pa."

"I aim to see to that," said Mr. Napier.

"Okay, Pa, we'll go to the drugstore instead," Bill said. "I'll take a hot fudge sundae if you're treating."

"Fine. We'd better hurry, too. It's nearly time to pick up your ma and sisters at the grocery."

CHAPTER 4

The City
Cousins

Bill has an aunt and uncle and three cousins named Begley who live in Middlesboro, Kentucky, fifteen miles south of Pineville. With a population of 14,000, Middlesboro is large for a mountain town.

Six-year-old Pat, eight-year-old Kay, and twelve-year-old Ricky Begley have fewer chores to do than the Napier children. Pat sets the table. Kay takes out the garbage. Ricky feeds the livestock: their hound, an old cat, and Charlie. Charlie is a twenty-year-old white horse. His owner has moved north and Charlie doesn't have to work anymore. But the owner pays Ricky to take care of the horse.

Although Middlesboro is in a valley, surrounded

by mountains, it is very like any other middle-sized town. The Begleys' next-door neighbors, the Wilsons, are not even from the mountains. They came to Middlesboro when Mr. Wilson took the job of manager at the Excello Shirt Factory. Excello Shirts is one of several new factories that have come to Middlesboro in the past few years. These factories provide jobs for the unemployed, and bring more money into the area.

Other factories in Middlesboro make mobile homes and wooden paneling for homes and offices. The Tenn-Flake plant, which makes paneling, uses mountain lumber as well as labor.

The Begleys get up around seven o'clock in the morning, so the children can get to school at eight. Because they live a little more than a mile from school, Pat, Kay and Ricky ride the school bus to school.

Pat and her friend Jane Wilson are both starting in the first grade. But Pat, like nearly all mountain children, was in the Head Start program last year. She

Pat, Kay, and Ricky Begley wait with other children to get on the school bus.

knows the alphabet and can read a little. Jane went to a kindergarten in the city and has not yet learned the alphabet. In most parts of the country, only the poorest children can attend government educational programs such as Head Start for pre-school boys and girls and Even Up for high school students. In Appalachia, they are open to everyone.

Mr. Begley works for the telephone company. Mrs. Begley works part-time as a secretary, and she leaves for her job after the children have left for school. She usually can be home before school is over. She likes working and she enjoys meeting people. Part of each week's salary is set aside for Pat, Kay, and Ricky's college fund. Neither Mr. nor Mrs. Begley was able to go to college, so they are determined that their children will.

Ricky's biggest interest now is sports. In the summer, he was on the Little League baseball team. Now, he is active in Little League football. Ricky is only in the seventh grade, and is not eligible for the high school football team. But he hopes to make the team when he is a junior or senior.

There was going to be a Little League football game at 5:00 P.M., and Ricky would play. Also, Kay was a cheerleader.

After school, Pat and Kay went shopping down-

Pat and Kay go shopping after school.

town. They each had a quarter to spend. First they stopped at the bakery and bought cream horns—light, biscuit-like pastry with a rich, creamy filling. Then they went down the street to Penney's and to Ward's, where they bought a quarter's worth of material to make doll clothes.

When they got home, it was nearly time for the football game. Ricky was talking to their mother in the kitchen. As she put her books away, Kay heard him talking about his Little League team, and about the high school team which would play Harlan on Friday. She knew some of the boys he named. A few were Negroes. While there are no Negroes around Red Bird Mission or other out-of-the-way parts of the mountains, some have moved into the larger towns. They are not always welcome, but they are a big help to the football teams.

"My goodness, it doesn't seem like football time yet," Mrs. Begley said. "It seems like the revival was only yesterday."

The revival had been in July. Baptists from miles around had gathered at the football field every night for a week. It was a social event as well as a religious one. Many people only see all their relatives once a year at revival time. Most of the Appalachian people are Baptists. They would never miss a week of inspired preaching and singing.

"It was a purty good revival," Mrs. Begley said.

"I mostly liked the singin'," Kay added. "And it was fun to see Bill and Nancy there."

The football game was exciting. Ricky and the rest of the team played hard. And with encouragement from Kay and the other cheerleaders, they won.

Football is a popular sport in the mountains and the grandstand was nearly full. Many grownups, not only parents, went to the game as soon as they were finished with their work. The announcer and score-keeper were reporters from the local radio station.

Mrs. Begley got up early on Sunday morning. When she saw that it would be a fine day, she promised the children they could go to Cumberland Gap for a picnic.

Kay cheers for Ricky's team at the Little League football game.

"This weather won't hold much longer," she said. "You can smell winter in the air. The trees are at the height of their color. I'll fry up some chickens and make some potato salad. Then we'll go to the Gap right after church."

"Oh, Mama, that'll be fine," said Pat.

"But I don't want you to miss church," added Kay.

"You start the chickens now," her husband suggested. "Then drive us to Sunday School. Come back and take the chickens off, and you can get back in time."

So that is what she did. When she got back to church, she found that her husband had promised to help take up the collection. So she sat with her family instead of singing in the choir as she had planned.

During the sermon, Pat looked around at her rela-

Ricky, #81, watches anxiously as the coach encourages the team.

tives in the church. Her mother has twelve brothers
and sisters. Three of them have moved away, one to
Virginia and the other two north to Detroit. The rest
were in church. Pat's grandfather, Papaw, still works in
the coal mines. He has worked there all his life. Pat's
grandmother, Mamaw, has some time to rest now that
her children are grown. But Mrs. Begley remembers
times when her mother kept house all day, ironed all
night, and polished the children's shoes first thing in
the morning, so they would look nice at school.

Pat looked around. There was Uncle Mickey; he
winked at her. He was her youngest uncle, only eigh-
teen years old. We're all so close, she thought. If anyone needs help, someone's always there. I wouldn't
want to be anywhere else or part of any other family.

Finally, the sermon ended and the Begleys joined
in singing the last hymn. After church, they talked to
their friends.

When they got home, they changed clothes and

Pat, sitting with her family in church,
listens to the sermon.

The Begleys look into Tennessee from the pinnacle of Cumberland Gap National Historical Park.

started for Cumberland Gap National Historical Park. The Gap is important in American history because it was the place where the pioneers first entered Kentucky. Although the Begleys are proud of their state's history, the park means more to them because it is a fine picnic place and has many trails for hiking.

After they had eaten, they started up the trail to the pinnacle. On the way, they stopped and explored one of the park's several caves.

As they stood at the pinnacle, Mr. Begley said, "It's a mighty purty land. And we're a fine family, too. I'm downright thankful."

CHAPTER 5

A Visit
with
Dan Sizemore

After school the following Friday, Bill met Dan as they had planned. They went on the big school bus to the intersection, then waited with four other children for the Jeep.

Bill was excited. "Do we really go for a ways along the creek?" he asked.

"Sure," Dan said. "There's no other way to get to our place. The road goes part way up the valley. Then you follow a gravel trail awhile longer, and purty soon you're in the creek bottom. The rest of them get off before then," he added, waving toward the others. "You have to hang on, but finally you get there."

As the Jeep started bumping into the hills, Bill found that he did have to hang on. The Jeep had a roof, but no sides. When it went fast, the wind was chilly. "I'm not sure I'd like riding in this all winter," Bill said.

"Oh, in the next few weeks I'll put the sides on," the driver told him. "There's a heater here, and it's not too cold."

"Not if you're wearing two coats," Dan added. "I've got six brothers and sisters living in the dorm 'cause it's so hard to get here. Once I'm in the seventh grade, I'll live in the dorm, too."

"Can you really get through here in all weather?" Bill asked the driver. The trail twisted and turned with the creek; mountains rose steeply on either side. The electric lines also followed the creek.

"Some of the trails are passable only when it's dry," the driver said. "But it takes a lot of ice to close this one."

"Hey, there goes a ground squirrel," Dan yelled. "I'd like to catch him and put him in my pocket." There

The road to the Sizemores' cabin leads through the creek.

are many ground squirrels, or chipmunks, in the mountains. Mountain boys like to catch them for pets. They tie a string around one of the ground squirrel's legs and fasten the string in a buttonhole. Then they put the ground squirrel in their shirt pocket.

Farther along, Dan called their attention to a brightly colored bird, a kingfisher, sitting on an electric wire.

Bill looked at the forests rising all around them. Although some leaves had fallen, the trees were still bright with color. "It's might purty," he said.

"You just come back along about January and see how purty it is," Dan said. "The leaves are all messy

Barren trees stand watch over the house in a hollow as winter descends on Appalachia.

under the snow, so you can't take a step without slip-
ping or getting icy water up to your ankles. The trees
look like old grave markers, all standing up waiting
for us."

"Why, Dan, where'd you hear that?" the driver
asked.

"My ma says it sometimes," Dan said. "She says
the coal for the fire won't light in bad weather, just out
of spite."

"Your mother has her hands full, there's no doubt
about that," the driver said.

"She only says it sometimes," Dan said. "Then
she's mostly just talkin'. Ma likes bein' alone with the

Dan crosses the footbridge on his way home.

trees and her flowers in the summer. She don't hold
with cityfied ways. Just so she gets down the creek to
church and prayer meetin'."

"Here we are, Bill. Let's go," Dan said as the Jeep
stopped.

At first there was no house in sight. But a foot
path led across a wooden bridge. Bill saw a whisp of
smoke, then a rooftop. A dog came to meet them. "Hi
ya, Rover," Dan said, patting him.

"That's home," Dan said, pointing toward the
smoke.

They thanked the driver, then started up the trail.
Before long, they came to the Sizemore cabin. About
half of it was built of logs. The rest was made of planks.

A porch stretched across the front of the cabin. Log posts supported a tin roof. Smoke was coming from the stone chimney at the center of the cabin. A man sat on the porch and a small child played in the dirt in front of the porch.

"This is the least 'un," Dan said, picking up the little girl. "She'll start in school next year. There's her and the six in the dorm and two brothers who are in Detroit working—they'll be home tomorrow, for a week—and my sister who finished school last year and me. With so many not home, there's lots of room for you tonight."

"Hey, Pa," Dan yelled. "This is Bill Napier."

"How do you do," Bill said as they walked up the porch steps.

The man did not stop rocking or smoking his pipe. He looked at Bill. Finally, he took the pipe from his mouth and said, "Howdy."

"Come on, let's see Ma," Dan said.

His mother and an older sister were tending a pot of green beans and potatoes seasoned with pork drippings, and a chicken, which were cooking on the stove. Bill could smell corn bread baking.

"Smells mighty good," he said. He looked around in the gloom and saw a coal stove, an open fireplace, a table and chairs, a couch, and several beds. A dim electric light bulb hung from the ceiling.

Mr. Sizemore looks out over his land with pleasure.

In spite of hard work and ten children, Mrs. Sizemore can smile at the world.

"So you're Bill Napier," Mrs. Sizemore said, turning from the stove. "Dan's talked about you enough. Well, you're welcome."

Dan hugged his youngest sister and put her down. "Go on back out till supper's ready," he said.

"Come on, Bill. You can put your things in the other room. Just toss them on the bed." He indicated one of the four that filled the room. "Then we'll feed the chickens and the cow."

Since the room was away from the fire, it was dark and chilly. Very little late afternoon light came through the windows. The Sizemore farm is in a hollow which runs north and south so the mountains cut off the sun except in the middle of the day.

"Most of us kids sleep here," Dan said, "even when everyone's home. It's warm enough under the quilts. And we've the stove for real cold weather." He pointed proudly at a round stove painted silver.

Bill had never seen a stove like it. "Pa made it out of old car wheel rims," Dan said. "He knows welding, and it heats real good."

"It looks mighty fine," Bill said. The Sizemores were certainly smarter than he had thought. They knew about the birds and animals in the woods. Dan's pa could make a stove out of wheel rims no one else wanted.

The Sizemore barn is nearly filled with hay and also has room for the cow. The chicken house on the left has a roof made from the hood of an old car.

The boys started toward the barn. It was built of logs, but the cracks in between were not filled in, so it didn't stop the wind. The chickens were kept in a shed at one end of the barn. Its roof seemed to be an old car hood. The main part of the barn was nearly filled with hay.

"Doesn't it get wet?" Bill asked.

"Not much. The mountain stops most of the wind from blowing the rain in our direction," Dan explained.

"Where's your cow?"

"Down the holler. We don't bring her in till the weather gets real bad."

They followed the creek past several acres of cornfields. As the hollow narrowed, they came to the beginning of the roughly fenced field where the cow was pastured. Bill heard her bell, but didn't see her.

"Thar she is, just past those trees." Dan pointed. "During the day she'll range four or five miles up the creek, but she's back here for feeding and milking." The cow came meekly up to him. As he squatted on the ground and milked her into a tin can, she ate the grain he had brought her.

"What kind of cow is she?" Bill asked.

"I don't know. But she gives us milk and a calf

Dan milks the family cow into a tin can. Milking her in the open saves driving her nearly a mile to the barn and back. The only problem is knowing where she will be at milking time.

every year. That's what counts," Dan said. He finished milking. "Let's get back. Ma'll have supper ready."

The family ate around the table in the living room. Dan's father kept glancing at Bill, but for a long time he said nothing.

He's curious, Bill thought, but he won't admit it.

Finally Mr. Sizemore spoke. "What's your pa do, boy?"

"We've a farm over from Beverly," Bill said.

"What's it grow?"

"Corn, a little over five acres of tobacco, some cane, hogs and dairy cows—Holsteins," Bill said.

"We raise young 'uns mostly." Mr. Sizemore chuckled.

"Hunting's what to do," he continued. "My pa hunted for a living. So did his pa. Now there's not much left. Some squirrels and rabbits for stew; no more'n a couple of deer a year. It's hardly worth going out."

"You goin' huntin' tomorrow, Pa?" Dan asked.

"Nope. Goin' to Cousin Tate's. Tradin' for his mule," Mr. Sizemore said. "Your pa hold with all this schoolin'?" he asked Bill.

"Yes, sir. My sister Margaret's goin' to Lexington next year to study to be a nurse."

"How wonderful!" Mrs. Sizemore said. "I wanted to be a nurse onct."

"Waste of time." Her husband snorted. "You can mend folks well as any nurse now. I can see sending the boys, but school just gives girls wrong notions. Wearing pants like a man!"

Dan's sister looked at her plate. She remembered the time her father caught her wearing slacks at school. She would never forget the whipping she had gotten.

"Play for us, Danny, will you?" Mrs. Sizemore asked.

Dan took an old, much-mended guitar from its hook on the wall and went out on the porch. The fam-

Singing is one of the Sizemores' favorite thing to do. Dan plays religious songs and old mountain ballads on the mended guitar.

ily and Bill followed him. Mrs. Sizemore carried the baby. The sun still struck the tops of the mountains. As the sun set and the stars came out, the Sizemores sang. Bill knew many of the songs. Some were church hymns. Others were ballads telling of long-dead kings and seafarers. Dan ended with the long, familiar ballad of hard-hearted Barb'ry Allen.

"Look, the least 'un's asleep," Mrs. Sizemore said.

"I almost am," her husband said. "Time for bed everyone."

The sun was shining in when Bill wakened. It must be nine o'clock at least, he thought, for the sun to be over the mountain. He could hear Dan and his mother talking in the next room.

"We sure could use a couple of squirrels for dinner," Mrs. Sizemore was saying.

"Has pa gone?" Dan asked her.

"Awhile ago. He won't be back till dark. You take care, boy."

Bill dressed and went into the next room, where Dan was eating a plateful of fried apples.

"Mornin', Bill," Mrs. Sizemore said. She put a plate of apples in front of him. "Sleep well?"

"Yes, thank you. Your quilts are nice and warm."

"I made most of those; my ma made the rest," Mrs. Sizemore said. "They last and last."

"Some of your patterns are like my ma's," Bill said.

"Well, we're all kin if you go back far enough. It's no wonder if our quilts are patterned alike," Mrs. Sizemore said. "Well, I'm off to hunt for eggs. You boys have fun."

After she left, Dan said, "Now's our chance. Let's get the gun."

"Didn't your ma say it was all right?"

"No. She wants the squirrels, but she wouldn't say so for fear of Pa. I've fed and milked the cow already, you sleepyhead. Let's go." He paused, then added, "She didn't know you were listening awhile ago, so don't let on.

Dan's chores also include drawing water from the well at the back door of the cabin. The tanks contain gas for the stove. Hollyhocks still bloom in the foreground.

"You see, Bill, this bit of a farm can't feed all of us now the game's mostly gone. We buy food stamps once a month, and we get the commodities." Commodities are surplus food the government distributes to poor people. "But Ma doesn't like that rice and stuff. Like as not we'll feed it to the chickens. Before the end of the month, we'll be out of food. And every chicken we kill, it'll be that many less eggs. So Ma wants those squirrels, and I'm man enough to get them for her."

For weeks, they had planned how they could get the rifle and go hunting, but now Bill was worried. "Dan, are you sure we ought to?" he asked.

"Sure, I do it all the time," Dan replied. "Haven't you ever shot a rifle?"

"Course I have, but Pa was always with me."

"Well, I'm goin' huntin'. You can come if you like," Dan answered.

Bill followed him as he got the gun and the shells for it. "Come on, now," Dan said. "Have you got your skinning knife?"

The boys went up the mountainside with Dan in the lead. Bill had to admit that Dan knew about hunting. He knew just how to find game and sneak up on it. Rover helped. He sniffed every tree till he found one with a squirrel in it.

"What kind of dog is he?" Bill asked.

Dan shoots a squirrel as
Bill watches.

"Dog," Dan said. "He comes in a direct line from the one that came across the mountains with my great grandpappy."

Before the day was over, they had killed and skinned three squirrels and a rabbit. They went home proudly.

As Dan was putting the gun away, the accident Bill had feared happened. Dan dropped the gun and it fired into his leg.

"Drat, I forgot the last shell," he muttered between his teeth.

"Dan, are you hurt? What can I do?" Bill asked.

"Get me a cobweb to stop the bleeding and find Ma," Dan said.

Bill pulled a spider's web down from a dark corner and put it on the wound. Mrs. Sizemore came running. She looked at Dan's leg, and seemed relieved. "You're lucky this time, boy," she said. "It missed the bone. But your pa'll tan your hide if he finds out." She got out some salve and tied a rag over the wound.

"Won't you go down to the hospital?" Bill asked Dan.

"Law, no. Ma can fix hurts better'n anyone down there. She's got cures for colds and stomach aches and most everything. She makes them from bark and roots and herbs," Dan said. "I'll take her over a doctor any time," he added as his mother came back into the room with another bandage.

"You won't tell Pa on me, will you, Ma?" he asked.

"I ought to. Don't you know not to put a loaded gun away? The least 'un could have gotten it," she scolded. Bill could see from her worried eyes that she cared about Dan's hurt leg, but she tried not to show it.

"Come on, boy, let's see how you can walk on it," she said. Dan could hobble around, although it hurt. "I reckon maybe your pa won't notice," she told him. "We'll get by this time."

Dan's brothers arrived from Detroit that afternoon, and in the excitement Mr. Sizemore didn't notice the limp. He did not seem disappointed that he had not bought the mule. He liked the squirrel stew. In fact the whole family enjoyed it, and so did Bill.

The next day, Sunday, Bill went with the Sizemores to their little church. Afterward, they ate more squirrel stew. Then Bill and Dan went down the creek to the walnut tree. A few walnuts had fallen. Using a stone, they beat off the pulpy green covering, then cracked and ate the nuts.

"Most of them, we let the skin dry and peel off before we crack them," Dan said. "But we kids rush a few like this. They're good, aren't they?"

"Sure are," Bill agreed. "You've a lot of good things out here."

"We like it," said Dan Sizemore.

CHAPTER 6

The Wilderness Travelers

After supper on Monday, Bill told his folks about his trip to the Sizemores'. When he finished, everyone was quiet for a minute. Then his mother spoke slowly.

"The Sizemores, they're folks out of their time. Their kin and mine walked into these mountains along the old Wilderness Road. My mamaw lived and died in a cabin like theirs; only they have electricity now.

"In fact, part of my kin are Sizemores. I don't know if we're kin to these. There are a lot of Sizemores. But my great-grandpappy took a Sizemore for his second wife. Or my great-great-grandpappy. It was early

Some roads are little more than Jeep trails, but the scenery is
beautiful.

in the last century. After he walked in, on the old Wilderness Road."

"Tell us about it, Ma," Bill begged, although he had heard the story a hundred times before.

So Mrs. Napier told the story of the settling of Kentucky. The pioneers walked along the Wilderness Trail. The men carried muskets; sometimes their wives did, too. The older children walked. The younger ones rode with the baggage on the family horse.

Most of these pioneers were born in Tennessee. Their parents had gotten that far and settled down. They came from Virginia, or "Virginny," as they called it, up the Warriors' Path. This road was first traveled by the Indians before the white men arrived in America. In the second half of the eighteenth century, the Indians guided the white men through the Cumberland Gap on the path which became the Wilderness Road.

"My great-grandpappy loaded up his rifle. He called his wife and young 'uns. He whistled up the dog and headed into Kaintuckee. Kaintuckee means dark and bloody ground in the Indians' talk. There were wars fought over this ground before the white men ever came through the Gap."

Bill's mother tells about the coming of the pioneers.

"The Indians must have regretted showing them the way," Margaret said slowly. "Especially after the white men bought it all."

"It wasn't a fair deal," Bill agreed. "The Cherokee leader, Attakullaculla, the Little Carpenter, must not have known what the land was worth. The whole Indian nation voted on it, but he was the leader. Later, they knew it was worth more than they were paid. But then it was too late to get it back, however they fought for it."

"That was before our kin came through the Gap," his mother continued. "The Indians were mostly gone when they came. Or else they married with the whites and people stopped thinking of them as Indians.

"Great-grandpappy married a Sizemore a year after he came to Jack's Creek, about five miles across the mountain from Beverly. His wife died that first winter, of the cold and of grieving for Tennessee."

"Why'd anyone grieve for Tenneesee, Ma?" Bill asked.

"Because it was her home, I reckon. And folks who aren't used to the mountains don't always take to them. They feel closed in."

This sort of thing happened to many pioneers. A wife died of a fever or in childbirth, leaving several children. Her husband had to marry soon in order to have a mother for his children. Often his second wife was a half-grown girl who bore him another ten or twelve children. And so the number of people in Kentucky increased.

Before the War Between the States began, the settlers in Appalachia had built log cabins and barns.

They had planted corn and tobacco on the hillsides and in the valleys along the creeks. They were busy raising cattle, hogs, chickens, and children. Those who lived away from the Wilderness Road were little concerned with the fighting. Sometimes soldiers stole hogs, but the only fighting in the area was around the Gap. After the

This farm has rich land. Between the bare trees in the center of the picture is the family burial plot. Many mountain people prefer to bury their dead at home rather than in a churchyard or a cemetery.

war, more settlers arrived. Some were former soldiers who liked the mountains they had seen when they were fighting for the Gap. Others were part of a general westward movement.

Some mountain people moved away, too. Most of the famous heroes of the early West, like Davy Crock-

The church nestled in a cluster of trees and the mountains themselves offer help in times of trouble.

ett and Sam Houston, were born in the mountains of Kentucky or Tennessee.

Mr. Napier looked up from his newspaper. "People still leave the mountains, looking for jobs in the cities. Then they're lonesome and unhappy when they get there. Look up the mountains. When you see a patch of poplars growing straight up, that used to be

plowed land. Some folks move away. Others stop working and let the government feed them. And others grow
more crops in the bottomlands, with fertilizer, and harvest the timber off the mountains.

"The mountains are a good place to live. You just
have to learn to do for yourself. These hills won't grow
crops by themselves. But if you work hard you can

make a good living on them. Coal isn't our only way of making money. Industry is coming into the mountains. Men, and women too, can learn to work in factories. Folks oughtn't to have to leave the mountains or live off of the government. You can make a living here, now. You kids will be able to do even better."

"Life is easier here now then it was when I was your age, Bill," Mrs. Napier said.

When the missionaries came to Bell County fifty years ago, they brought schools as well as religion. Until then, hardly anyone could write his name. Soon afterward, people started to buy radios. They could listen to what was happening in the outside world. Gradually, more and more people were able to get electricity. Now, even the people who are farthest from roads, like the Sizemores, can have electric lights.

"When I was a child," Mrs. Napier went on, "there were no roads at all out here. It took a whole day to get to Pineville on horseback. After a while, the state and the missionaries were able to clear out Jeep tracks in the creeks. Then came gravel roads, and finally pavement."

Because of the roads, the whiskey stills and the family feuds which were common even twenty years ago are nearly gone. Law officers can get from Pineville to Beverly in twenty minutes. This discourages both the making of illegal liquor and the shooting of neighbors.

"The only time feuds are apt to flare up is election time," Mrs. Napier said. "But even then, folks are fighting it out more with ballots than bullets.

"The hospital's helped us, too," she continued. "Women don't die in childbirth anymore. The doctors set broken bones and cure fevers. Shots and vaccinations stop the bad fevers before they can get started.

"Life's better in the mountains now. I think it'll keep on being good. Some of our kin moved farther west. Maybe you will, too. But the sun's mighty purty hanging over Chigger Mountain in the morning."

The wintery fogs that come before it's cold enough to snow are purty, too, Bill thought. After the first of the year, there will be some weeks with too much snow to get to town, and a few days the school bus won't even run. By March, the ground is thawed. Trees start to bud. Then Pa and Jake will be plowing. The forest is so beautiful then. The wild dogwood, redbud, and mountain laurel will still flower well after Easter. After that will come all the wild flowers.

Then in summer, I can go barefoot in Red Bird

The sun setting over Chigger Mountain and Red Bird Creek.

Creek, looking for tadpoles, when Pa doesn't need my help. Finally comes harvest. By Thanksgiving, the crops are all in; the tobacco sold. Ma will have canned, frozen, and pickled the vegetables.

"Time for bed, Bill. There's school tomorrow." His mother's voice broke his thoughts. But he knew why mountain children didn't want to leave the mountains. Pat, Kay, and Ricky, all the Sizemores, Margaret and Nancy, and Bill himself. The life can be hard, but none of them could feel happy anywhere else. The mountains are home.

Bill hugged his father and mother especially hard. He even kissed his sisters.

"Good night," he said.

Index